I0014824

Kubernetes Vs. Docker

A Step-by-Step Guide to Learn and Master Kubernetes and Docker

© Copyright 2019 by BRAYDEN SMITH - All rights reserved.

This eBook is provided with the sole purpose of providing relevant information on a specific topic for which every reasonable effort has been made to ensure that it is both accurate and reasonable. Nevertheless, by purchasing this eBook you consent to the fact that the author, as well as the publisher, are in no way experts on the topics contained herein, regardless of any claims as such that may be made within. As such, any suggestions or recommendations that are made within are done so purely for entertainment value. It is recommended that you always consult a professional prior to undertaking any of the advice or techniques discussed within.

This is a legally binding declaration that is considered both valid and fair by both the Committee of Publishers Association and the American Bar Association and should be considered as legally binding within the United States.

The reproduction, transmission, and duplication of any of the content found herein, including any specific or extended information will be done as an illegal act regardless of the end form the information ultimately takes. This includes copied versions of the work both physical, digital and audio unless express consent of the Publisher is provided beforehand. Any additional rights reserved.

Furthermore, the information that can be found within the pages described forthwith shall be considered both accurate and truthful when it comes to the recounting of facts. As such, any use, correct or incorrect, of the provided information will render the Publisher free of responsibility as to the actions taken outside of their direct purview. Regardless, there are zero scenarios where the original author or the Publisher can be deemed liable in any fashion for any damages or hardships that may result from any of the information discussed herein.

Additionally, the information in the following pages is intended only for informational purposes and should thus be thought of as universal. As befitting its nature, it is presented without assurance regarding its prolonged validity or interim quality. Trademarks that are mentioned are done without written consent and can in no way be considered an endorsement from the trademark holder.

Table of Contents

Kubernetes

A Step-by-Step Guide to Learn and Master Kubernetes

Docker

A Step-by-Step Guide to Learn and Master Docker

Kubernetes

A Step-by-Step Guide to Learn

and Master Kubernetes

Introduction

I want to thank you and congratulate you for downloading *Kubernetes: A Step-by-Step Guide to Learn and Master Kubernetes*. This book contains proven steps and strategies on how to effectively use Kubernetes for various purposes.

The steps, examples, practical methods, and host of background information provide readers with strategies to operate Kubernetes in the most effective manner possible. Given that the nature of the Kubernetes platform is expansive and intricate, there is a conspicuous lack of text available to readers striving to acquire more information about the platform. Finally, this has changed.

With this text, all of the seemingly complicated and intricate facets of Kubernetes is presented in clear, informative detail that will facilitate a greater understanding of the platform as a whole. Also, each chapter is carefully constructed so that readers of all levels of familiarity with the platform are able to comprehend and appreciate the information therein. Given the rather complicated nature of the Kubernetes platform, it is in the best interest of users across all levels of familiarity and ability to learn the methods and strategies presented within this text.

One of the most beneficial aspects of this text is the problem-solving keys that are presented. Indeed, readers will acquire extensive knowledge about how to fix any of the most prevalent and persistent problems that are encountered when operating the Kubernetes platform.

The text starts off by presenting the various ways that Kubernetes operates, including how to maximize the functionality and performance of the platform. From there, deployment, pods, and services are presented in sequence with detailed information about configuration and other facets of the areas of Kubernetes. Thereafter, the chapters contain in-depth knowledge about Kubernetes extensions, Client Libraries, and Design Patterns.

Infused with the full expanse of modern, state-of-the-art information pertaining to the entire Kubernetes platform, readers will enjoy a pronounced advantage when operating it for various purposes and projects.

Thanks again for downloading this book. I hope you enjoy it!

Chapter 1: How Kubernetes Operates

As a portable open-source platform that is also extensible, Kubernetes is excellent for effective management of multiple workloads and services that are containerized. In addition, Kubernetes allows for automation, along with declarative configuration, through its platform.

While Kubernetes offers many different and useful features across its platform, it can be thought of in three different ways:

1) Platform with micro-services
2) Container platform
3) Portable cloud platform

Notably, Kubernetes offers a management environment that is container-centric. In this way, Kubernetes manages networking and computing capabilities, as well as an extensive infrastructure for storage for user-friendly workloads. As a result, Kubernetes allows for the simplistic capability of a Platform as a Service (PaaS), along with Infrastructure as a Service (IaaS). What's more, Kubernetes facilitates increased portability among providers.

While Kubernetes enhances performance and functionality, there remain many situations that benefit from newer features. For instance, workflows that are specific to applications are able to be streamlined in order to augment the velocity of the developer. Impromptu orchestration usually needs intricate automation. This is the reasoning for Kubernetes being developed to be a platform that builds an arena of components and tools that ameliorate the process of scaling, deploying, and managing several different programs.

Moreover, labels give users the ability to organize and optimize resources in whatever manner they desire. Also, additions let users embed different resources with custom information. This allows users to more easily facilitate each workflow and enable a simpler method for tools of management to checkpoint state. It is also important to consider that the Kubernetes plane of control is developed on the exact same APIs that remain accessible to users. Not to mention, users are also able to write and develop their own controllers, including schedules, with the same APIs that can also be targeted by a command-line application.

In addition to detailing the sprawling benefits and features offered by Kubernetes, it is also equally important and beneficial to present and consider what Kubernetes does *not* offer users. For example, Kubernetes *cannot* be categorized as a traditional PaaS platform that is all-inclusive. As Kubernetes is an application that is operated at a container level, as opposed to hardware, Kubernetes gives features that are aligned with PaaS systems. These include deployment, logging, and scaling, to name a few. Nonetheless, Kubernetes is not inflexible—therefore, solutions that are "default" are thereby optional. Not to mention, Kubernetes gives solid foundational tools for creating different developer platforms—however, it sustains flexibility in important areas.

While not restricting the many forms of applications that it supports, Kubernetes is designed to support a multitude of workloads that are diverse. These include stateful, stateless, as well as workloads that are designed for processing complex data. Additionally, Kubernetes is an excellent choice for applications that run in containers.

Kubernetes is capable of source code deployment and will not allow users to put together their own unique applications. However, it will not provide users with services that are application-level, such as data processing frameworks, for example. These features can be operated on Kubernetes or are able to be accessed by applications operating through Kubernetes using portable features. Open Service Broker is an example one of these mechanisms that Kubernetes can be operated on.

It is also important to note that Kubernetes is not useful for alerting, dictating or monitoring solutions. Instead, Kubernetes facilitates any integrations in a manner consistent with proof of concept, along with many ways to collect and even export different metrics. Not to mention, Kubernetes is also insufficient for mandating and facilitating configuration systems and languages. Rather, Kubernetes will offer declarative API that could very likely be used for arbitrary systems and declarative specification.

If you are attempting to adopt a machine configuration that is relatively comprehensive or to use a platform for maintenance and self-healing systems, you will find that Kubernetes is not helpful for these purposes either. In addition, Kubernetes is not an orchestration system. Indeed, Kubernetes will eliminate orchestration altogether. Given that the technical and working definition for orchestration is executing an organized and designed workflow, Kubernetes is made up of a combined set of comparable and independent systems that continue to push a system's current state closer to the state that is desired.

Granted, it should not matter too much how you move through steps A to C; in other words, centralized control is not needed when using Kubernetes. As a result, you will end up with a system that is much easier to implement, and it will also be more powerful.

While it may certainly seem like there are many limitations in the way that Kubernetes operates, keep in mind that Kubernetes eliminates many formerly mandatory operation approaches, such as orchestration which requires that steps be executed following an "A to C" framework. In this way, Kubernetes expedites the process through which processes are executed, saving you time and effort.

So, why should you even consider using containers? The traditional method of deploying application systems was through installing applications onto a host that is using the operating system's package. As a result, this carried the unique advantage of entwining many different aspects such as libraries, executables, and life cycles with one another along with the OS host. In this traditional approach, users were able to construct virtual machine images to acquire rollbacks and rollouts. However, virtual-machine images are not portable and are heavyweight.

In the modern approaches, containers are deployed through operating-system virtualization as opposed to hardware. Notably, modern containers are separates from the host as well as one another. In this way, these modern containers have filesystems that are unique to them, are unable to view the processes of other filesystems, and, lastly, the computational resource of the new containers are able to be effectively bounded.

Also, new containers are far easier to construct than virtual-machines and are more portable along OS systems and clouds due to being decoupled from underlying infrastructure as well as the host filesystem. As most containers are relatively small in stature and operate at a fast rate, every container image can contain its own application within it. As a result, this relationship between the container image and application will unlock the full potential of containers. Through containers, immutable images in containers are able to be developed at a release/build time as opposed to deployment rate of time, because each of these applications is not required to be put together using the entirety of the application stack, and it does not need to be tethered to the overall infrastructure environment.

Producing container images in build and release time allows for an environment that is far more consistent and that can be carried from each stage to the next, such as from development to production, for instance. In the same way, containers are much more transparent when compared to virtual-machines—this allows for management and closer monitoring. What's more, this is even truer when considering that the container's lifecycle is managed specifically by the infrastructure instead of hiding from within the container by a process supervisor.

Lastly, with only a single application for each container, managing each container is analogous to managing the specific deploying of each application. We will examine the deployment of Kubernetes in more depth in Chapter 2.

From a general standpoint, Kubernetes can be seen as allowing for new patterns of design, much like design patterns that are object-oriented but for applications that are containerized. Indeed, the emergence of design patterns from within containerized architectures is not the least shocking, as most containers do provide a lot of that benefits and upsides as many software objects with regard to packaging, reuse, and even abstraction.

Further, due to containers usually engaging with one another through HTTP and other formats that are broadly available, such as JSON, the unique upsides are able to be provided in a manner that is independent of language.

As Kubernetes persists with bringing over 10 years of experience with Borg to the community of open source networking, the aim of Kubernetes is facilitating applications that are "cloud-active," as well as ensuring that application operations and deployment reliable and at scale.

Moreover, Kubernetes' projects and dedication to documenting all of their ideas surrounding design patterns for services that are container-based, including Kubernetes' allowing of such patterns, is the initial step in this direction.

What's more, Kubernetes is committed to working alongside practitioner and academic groups and communities to codify and identify other patterns, with the intention of assisting containers with fulfilling the dedication of fostering more reliability and simplicity to the whole lifecycle of software- ranging from operation to deployment and development.

Chapter 2: Kubernetes Deployment

Kubernetes Deployment, as per the official documentation, involves the user "describing the desired state in a Deployment object, through which the Deployment controller changes the actual state to the desired one at a controlled rate."

Prior to examining how Deployments specifically operate, it is important to consider that Kubernetes is an object store that also has code that is specifically designed to interact with the objects. Moreover, every object that is stored has 3 components: specification, current status, and metadata. The user's role is to provide the metadata, along with a specification where the desired state of each object is thereby described. Kubernetes works to ensure that this desired state manifests.

With regard to deployments, Kubernetes deployments oversee services that are stateless and can run on your cluster, rather than StatefulSets, which tend to manage stateful services. The purpose of deployments is to ensure that sets of identical pods are kept running and are then upgraded in a manner that is controlled. This is to say that rolling updates are performed by default.

You should also note that "Replicas" in key names refers to the specific number of pods that are replicated, as opposed to the number of ReplicaSets. Also, consider the following with regard to Kubernetes deployments:

- **Replicas** are copied directly from the spec. In a brief interval, you can read a deployment specifically where spec.replicas are not congruent with status.replicas.

- **availableReplicas** refers to the number of pods that are readily prepared for some time (minReadySeconds). As a result, this will certainly assist with preventing flapping of state.

- **unavailableReplicas** refers to the overall number of pods that you should ensure are present, minus the number of pods that have yet to be produced.

- **updatedReplicas** are the overall number of pods that are reachable by this specific form of deployment, as long as they match the spec template.

- **readyReplicas** are the total pod numbers that can be reached from deployment all the way through each of the replicas.

Kubernetes employs Conditions in many different areas of its platform. These are all lists of condition objects. Keep in mind that the very minimal object will contain a status, type, and reason.

Once you are equipped with a Kubernetes cluster, you are then able to deploy all of the containerized applications along with it fully. In order to do this, you will have to formulate a configuration of Kubernetes Deployment. In addition, the Deployment will inform Kubernetes on how to produce and update different instances of the system. After you have finally produced a Deployment, the Kubernetes master will schedule each mentioned applications and systems onto Nodes within the cluster.

Thereafter, when these application and system instances are produced, a Kubernetes Deployment Controller will begin to monitor each of those instances. Moreover, if the Node hosting a particular instance is deleted, the Deployment controller will then replace it. This is important because it will provide a mechanism of self-healing that effectively addresses machine failure as well as maintenance.

Prior to pre-orchestration, scripts for installation tended to be used primarily for starting certain applications. However, they would not allow for effective recovery from machine failure. Through simultaneously and independently producing application instances and maintaining their operation along Nodes, Deployments with Kubernetes offers a very different approach to management of applications.

Interestingly, you are able to manage and even create a Deployment quite easily by utilizing the Kubernetes command line, which is referred to as Kubectl. Further, Kubectl makes use of the Kubernetes API to engage with clusters.

When you begin to produce a Deployment, you will be required to be specific with the container image that you choose to incorporate for your application as well as the overall number of replicas that you wish to run. Also, you can adjust this information afterword simply by updating Deployment.

Remember that Kubernetes will automate deployment, application scaling, and operations. However, the goal of Kubernetes does not only pertain to system management, but it is also designed to assist all developers as well. In other words, Kubernetes should ease the process through which distributed services and applications running within datacenter and cloud environments are written. In order to trigger this, Kubernetes makes two primary designations: Kubernetes will define an API for applications that are containerized to engage with the particular management platforms, along with defining a certain API for administrators so that they can perform particular actions for effective management.

While much of the work on defining an API for applications that are containerized to interact with management platforms are still in the process of being refined, there have been some key features that have stemmed from this process already:

- The Kubernetes mechanism of **Graceful Termination** offers containers an increased amount of time before it is terminated, this may be due to a maintenance node drain, or even an update that is occurring on a rolling basis, and or a multitude of other reasons. This will allow an application to be shut down more efficiently without any hindrances.

- **ConfigMap** lets applications read configuration directly from Kubernetes as opposed to employing flags that are command-line.

- **Readiness probes** ensure a configurable application HTTP endpoint, although other forms are also supported. This allows for determining whether the container in question is ready to be the recipient of traffic and whether it is even alive. Moreover, this specific function and response will determine if Kubernetes will restart the container and or decide to incorporate it within the pool of load balancing for its service.

Deployments stand for a distinct collection of identical and multiple Pods devoid of any unique identities. It is important to note that a Deployment operates many different replicas of certain applications. This also replaces, in an automatic manner, replaces all particular occurrences when using the platform or else it will not respond. As a result, Deployments make sure that at least one, but likely more, of the instances that you encounter with your application are made available to serve all requests from the user.

Now, Deployments employ a template for Pods. This contains a certain specification for Pods. Moreover, the Pod distinction will ultimately determine the manner in which every Pod appears. This includes certain applications that are to operate within containers, along with which volumes the Pods are to mount. Once a Deployment's Pod template is altered or morphed in some particular way, brand new Pods will be produced in an automatic fashion, one at a time.

Now, deployments are perfectly tailored for applications that are stateless and that employ only ReadOnlyMany features and volumes that are tethered to various replicas but are far from being a good fit for workloads that utilize ReadWriteOnce volumes. On the other hand, for stateful applications utilizing ReadWriteOnce features, StatefulSets is the best feature to use. These sets are designed to unload clustered and stateful applications that preserve information and data to storage that is persistent. Compute Engine is an example of this.

Producing deployments can be achieved by utilizing a few different commands. To name just a few, these include: Kubectl create, Kubectl run, and Kubectl apply. One these are produced, the Deployment will make sure that the user's desired amount of Pods will operate effectively, without glitches, and are available everywhere.

Moreover, Deployment will immediately replace all Pods

that reach failure or are removed from nodes.

Updating deployments can be achieved by making certain alterations to Deployment's Pod template feature. Enforcing certain changes to this feature field will immediately cause a rollout of an update. In a default manner, whenever a Deployment is triggered and whenever an update ensues, the Deployment will halt the Pods and then diminish the overall amount of Pods to zero. Thereafter, it will terminate and drain the Pods altogether. The Deployment will then utilize the updated Pod template to raise brand new Pods.

Old Pods will not be taken out of the system until there are a sufficient amount of newer Pods that are up and operating. New Pods will not be produced until enough of the older Pods have been taken out. If you wish to view which Pods, and in what order, are brought forth and then removed from the system, users can run certain functions that the platform will provide.

Deployments make sure that, at the very least, one less than the total number of desired replicas is operating. In this instance, only one Pod, at the most, will be unavailable.

Finally, the life cycle and status of Deployments is worth deeper consideration. Notably, Deployments will be found in one of 3 different states at any particular time: Failed, Completed or Progressing.

A Failed state demonstrates that the Deployment has found one or more problems inhibiting it from finishing tasks that it has been assigned. Granted, some of these causes will include permissions and or quotas that are not sufficient, along with runtime errors, limit ranges or image pull errors. A

Next, a Completed state suggests that Deployment has effectively finished all tasks that it has been assigned. In addition, this state indicates that all of the Pods are operating with the latest variation and are currently available. Also, this state suggests that there are no old Pods that are up and running.

Lastly, a progressing state suggests that the Deployment is currently in the process of performing particular tasks, such as scaling Pods and or bringing them up to the fore.

If users wish to investigate further about the specific causes of a Deployment's failure, they can examine all of the messages within the field labeled status:conditions.

Chapter 3: Kubernetes Pods

A pod can be referred to as a group of one or more containers with a shared network or storage, along with a certain specification for ways to operate each of the said containers.

The contents of a pod tend to consistently be found, scheduled, and operated/run within a context that is shared. Moreover, a pod will model application-specific logical host—this means that it will contain at least one application container coupled together within a pre-container system. These pre-container systems are operated within the same virtual or physical machine—thus, they would also then be executed within the same logical host.

Despite Kubernetes supporting many more container operating times than compared to Docker, the latter system is the better-known runtime. Therefore, it is more helpful for our purposes to describe pods using Docker terms.

A kubernetes pod operates within a shared context. Also, it is a Linux namespaces collection, cgroups, as well as many additional facets of isolation. You may notice that these are the exact same things that will isolate a Docker container.

Inside of the context of a pod, individual applications will very likely apply more sub-isolations. In addition, containers inside of a pod share a port space along with an IP address. These can be found by each other using localhost. These can also be controlled and communicated through standard inter-process communications such as SystemV as well as shared memory through POSIX.

For different pods, containers will have unique IP addresses and will not be able to communicate via IPC unless a special configuration is present. Not to mention, these containers tend to communicate with one another through the IP addresses of pods.

In these pods, shared volumes will be accessible to many applications—these volumes are designed as belonging to a pod and can also be easily mounted onto the filesystem of each application. With regard to Docker constructs, each pod is specifically designed as being in one Docker container collection within shared volumes as well as namespaces. Similar to individual container applications, pods are not generally considered durable systems and entities.

If a node gives out, pods that are assigned to that node are thereby arranged to be deleted. Rather than each pod being rescheduled to a brand new node, it is replaced by another pod that is identical to it. The same name can be kept for the new pod; however, a new UID will be required.

When something, such as a volume, for example, has a similar lifespan as a pod, this means that it will continue to exist so long as the pod with the UID also exists. If, for whatever reason, the pod is deleted or removed, despite providing an exact auxiliary, your related volume, for instance, will be obliterated then produced brand new.

A pod diagram will contain a web server as well as a file-pulling feature that utilizes a volume for shared storage found between each container.

Pod Motivation

Pods are a configuration of patterned and cooperating processes that form a unit of service that is cohesive. Moreover, these pods will simplify the management and the deployment of applications by offering a high-level abstraction that superseded the level offered by their constituent applications.

Remember that pods are always serving as units of deployment, replication, and horizontal scaling. In addition, there are a few features that are managed automatically for containers within a pod—these include resource sharing, co-location, shared fate, and dependency management.

Among pods' constituents, pods facilitate sharing of data as well as communication. The network namespace will also be shared among apps found within them—similar to the mechanism that governs Internet Protocol as well as port space. As a result, they are able to more easily find and communicate with each other when they are using localhost. Consequently, all pod applications are required to coordinate how they use ports.

Every pod has its own IP address within a flat shared space used for networking that is also equipped with full communication with physical computers, as well as all of the other pods across a network. Note that the hostname will be set to the name of the pod for the application containers that exist within the pod.

Along with defining the container applications that operate within each pod, pods also specify a shared set of volumes. Further, volumes allow for data to persist through all restarts of a container along with being shared among all of a pod's applications.

A helpful benefit of pods is that you can easily utilize them in hosting app stacks that are vertically integrated, whose fundamental goal lies in aiding co-managed as well as co-located systems, which then include:

- cache managers, management systems for content, loaders for data and files
- snapshotting, compression, and log and checkpoint backup
- event publishers, data change watchers

Individual pods are not designed to operate instances simultaneously within a shared application.

So, you might be wondering why you can't just run multiple programs at the same time within a single container? (Docker container)

Well, there are 3 primary reasons. First, for easing the use of the application. This is to say that users do not necessarily need to operate their own process managers, along with worrying about certain propagation for exit codes and certain signals.

Also, for reasons of transparency, letting the containers that can be found inside the pods to be more present in the overall infrastructure allows process management as well as monitoring resources. Moreover, this allows more convenient operation for all users of the system.

Also, separating and or decoupling software dependencies is another reason. Individual containers are able to be redeployed, rebuilt and even versioned under certain conditions. In addition, Kubernetes might even allow for supporting live updates pertaining to individual containers. Lastly, efficiency is another why you cannot run multiple programs the exact same time in a single container, which is due to the fact that as the infrastructure attracts more responsibility, containers will also be lighter in weight.

Lack of Durability in Pods?

Notably, pods are not typically intended to necessarily be used as entities that are more durable and long-lasting. This is because they will not be able to persist through failures pertaining to scheduling, along with evictions and node failures. For the record, other evictions include not having resources (or even node maintenance, for this particular instance). Generally speaking, people should refrain from producing pods directly. Instead, they should focus on using controllers for singletons, such as Deployments, for instance. The benefit of the controller is that they induce the redevelopment of oneself. Even more, controllers such as StatefulSet will provide additional effective support to pods that are stateful.

The effective usage of APIs, in terms of being your main customer-dealing primitive, proves to be quite typical with respect to other cluster arranging mechanisms.

Effective use of APIs (collective) as the main user-facing primitive is typical among many cluster scheduling systems.

Also, a kubernetes pod can be revealed as a primitive to ensure the following:

- Pod-level operations support (devoid of having to "proxy" through API controllers)
- Decoupling of lifetime pod from controller lifetime (this includes bootstrapping as well)
- Exposing the pod to facilitate "pluggability" of controller and scheduler
- Cluster-level functionality

Pods are the tiniest and most rudimentary of the deployable objects within the entire Kubernetes platform. Moreover, it signifies an instance of a running process that is occurring within a cluster that you are using.

Notably, Pods carry at least one or more containers within them. These often include Docker containers. Whenever a Pod operates a few containers at the same time, these containers will be managed as singular entities that are tethered to a Pod's resources. In most cases, operating multiple containers within a Pod is used only in advanced instances.

Users should consider Pods to be isolated and self-contained "logical hosts." These will carry systemic needs of whichever applications that it is assigned to serve. Moreover, a Pod's overall purpose is to operate only one instance of an application on a cluster. Nevertheless, users are not recommended to produce individualized Pods. Rather, they are well-advised to produce a collection of Pods that are identical to one another in order to run a particular application effectively.

What's more, replica Pods are overseen and produced by a specific *controller;* a Deployment is an example of a controller. The Ain responsibility of controllers is to effectively manage and oversee lifespan of Pods, while also performing something called horizontal scaling. While one may consider having Pods be interacted with in order to inspect, troubleshoot or even debug, controllers are strongly recommended for managing a Pod.

Pods, running on nodes within a cluster, will remain tethered to the said node until the full expanse of the process has been completed. Then, the Pod will be deleted and evicted from this node because of a lack of resources, or if the node fails. In the case of the latter, a Pod that is on the node will be immediately deleted.

Terminating Pods

As pods tend to be more representative of running certain processes that are on nodes with the cluster, you should allow these particular processes to be terminated once they are not needed any longer, as opposed to being deleted while comprising of some kill signal as well as not being given the opportunity of cleaning up.

It is also important to note that users should be capable of requesting immediate deletion as well as knowing when processes are to be terminated. Also, users should also be capable of making sure that all of their deletes are completed and followed through with.

Whenever a certain user wants to delete a pod, the system will thereafter record whatever the intended grace period is prior to the pod being allowed to be killed off. In addition, this must occur before your containers' main processes receive the TERM signal.

Upon having a certain time elapses, these processes then receive your KILL signal, thus enabling your API server's pod to be obliterated. In case that you reignite your container (or what's referred to as Kubelet) when anticipating the processes' cancellation, this deletion process, as well as your grace period, is going to get stopped.

Below is an example of a flow:

1. The consumer directs a particular order of obliterating the Pod; the period of grace here is 30 seconds.

2. Within your API server, a Pod is continually renewing even upon surpassing the time that it is deemed to be dead.

3. Your Pod appears as to be Terminating when it is posted within client commands.

4. In conjunction with step #3, whenever the Kubelet views that a certain Pod is marked as having been terminated (or in the process), given that the duration pertaining to step #2 is already fixed, the process of terminating your Pod will then start.

5. If one of the Pod's containers has uniquely defined a preStop hook, it is then imprinted within a container. If, for instance, the particular preStop hook is continuing to operate once the grace period has ended, the 2nd step is then imprinted along with a relatively small grace period (extended by nearly 3 seconds).

6. Next, the container is delivered the TERM signal. Keep in mind that not every container within the Pod will automatically receive the TERM signal at the exact same moment and might even need a preStop hook if they must be shut down in a certain order.

7. In conjunction with step #3, Pod is to be immediately removed from each endpoint list for service, and will not be considered germane to the set of operating pods for replication controllers. It is important to note that the Pods that shutdown incrementally will not be able to serve traffic because load balancers will remove them from all of their locations.

8. While the grace period is no longer operating, any of the processes that are continuing to operate within the Pod end up being terminated using SIGKILL.

9. Finally, your Kubelet is eventually going to complete the deletion of your POD from your API server through establishing a zero grace period, which signifies instantaneous removal. Thereafter, your Pod is then nowhere to be found in your API or is already inaccessible to your client.

Another important note relating to pods is their force deletion. This can adequately refer to the pods' removal from your cluster state as well as etcd. Moreover, whenever this happens, your kubelet's approval is no longer necessitated by your apiserver.

This will then remove your pod right away in order to give way to a brand new one with a similar name. Those established to be deleted right away, particularly the ones on your node, will still be afforded a short period of grace prior to being force deleted.

Granted, users should note that this may prove harmful to many of your pods. Thus, caution is necessary when they are performed.

Pod containers also incorporate a privileged mode. As per Kubernetes version 1.1, this particular mode is activated through employing a pod's privileged flag right on your container spec's SecurityContext. Notably, it's especially helpful in getting containers to employ abilities aligned with Linux, such as manipulating the accessing devices and network stack.

Processes that are in the container tend to retrieve nearly the same privileges that ones that are external to the container also have. In the aforementioned mode, writing volume and network plugins are bound to be simpler as individual pods free from needing to be stacked within your kubelet.

Chapter 4: Kubernetes Services

A kubernetes service is generally considered a REST object. Indeed, this is very similar to a kubernetes pod. In the same way as all of the REST objects, a SERVICE is signified by having the ability to get included in your apiserver in order to produce an entirely new instance. Say, you have a set of PODs and that all of them expose your port 9376 then possess an "app=MyApp" label.

This particular specification is able to produce a brand new Service object that is labeled as "my-service" that will then target TCP port 9376 on any specific Pod that carries the label of "app=MyApp."

Notably, the said Service is then to be given a specific IP address, which is also referred to as "cluster IP." This is also used by Service proxies. Keep in mind that a Service is uniquely capable of mapping an incoming port to any targetPort in the system. In practice, your targetPort is to be given value identical to that of your port field.

Interestingly, the targetPort can refer to the same of a port in the backend Pods. In this way, the targetPort can be a string. The specific number that is thereafter assigned to that name does not have to be the same in each of the backend Pods.

Consequently, this will provide more deployment flexibility and will allow for Services to evolve. To exemplify, you are able to alter the number of the pros that each pod exposes in the subsequent version of your software backend. This can be done without having to break clients.

Take note that kubernetes Services are capable of supporting protocols for TCP, SCTP, and UDP. The default setting is TCP.

Services commonly abstract kubernetes Pods' access; however, they are also capable of abstracting other backend forms. For instance, you should aim to have a database cluster (external) during production; however, when testing, you should use databases that are your own. Also, you should strive to aim your service to a different service that can be found within another Namespace, or even within another cluster altogether.

It is important to note that because you're transferring all of the existing workloads to kubernetes, several backends will then operate externally to it. Now, considering this, you are able to define a certain service without also including a selector.

Proxy-Mode

With regard to this mode, kube-proxy keeps watch over the Kubernetes master for the specific elimination of Endpoints as well as Service objects. This then enables access to a port that is selected randomly on your local node for each specific Service.

Note that any particular connections related to this port are to be proxied to one of the backend Pods of the Service— just as it is reported in Endpoints. Any backend Pod that is used will be determined in accordance with your SessionAffinity for each Service.

Finally, this will automatically install iptables rules designed to encapsulate all of the traffic to the Service's virtual cluster along with the Port and will redirect all of the traffic to the proxy port responsible for proxying the backend Pod. Notably, the selection of the backend is round-robin (this is done by default).

There are particular environmental variables for Kubernetes Services that should be considered as well. For example, whenever a Pod is operated on a Node, the kubelet will then add a stack of environment variables for every active Service in the system. Moreover, it will then support both of the Docker links.

Thankfully, this process will not require any order. Instead, any Service that a specific Pod is trying to acquire access to will have to be produced *prior* to the Pod itself. If not, the variables within the environment will be unpopulated. However, this restriction does not apply to DNS systems.

With regard to DNS systems, it is strongly recommended (though optional) add-on for a cluster is a DNS server. The DNS server will survey the Kubernetes API for all new Services and will then create a stack of DNS records for all of them as well. If, for instance, DNS is made accessible within your entire cluster, every single Pod will then have the capability of performing name resolution of all Services. on their own.

Headless Services

On certain occasions, however, you will not be required to incorporate load-balancing and single service IPs. For the said instance, it is necessary to produce "headless" services by providing the destination "None" to your cluster IP.

The said option then facilitates all developers in limiting Kubernetes systems coupling by allowing more autonomy to perform discoverer on their own.

Applications will still be able to use a pattern of self-registration. Also, all other forms of discovery systems can be built rather easily on this specific API.

As such, for the said Services, a cluster IP will not be allocated as kube-proxy and will not handle any of these services for you—and the platform will not conduct proxying and load balancing.

The specific way in which DNS is configured will entirely hinge on if the service contains selectors that are defined.

For defined selectors, endpoints controller will create Endpoints records within the API. Also, they will modify the DNS configuration so that it returns A records pointing to Pods backing the Service.

Devoid of selectors, Endpoints controller will not produce

records for Endpoints. Nonetheless, the DNS system will configure and search for the following:

CNAME records for ExternalName-type services.

Publishing Services

Now, for certain aspects of the application that you are using, front ends are an example, you might wish to reveal a particular Service directly on an IP address that is external (located on the outside of a cluster).

Kubernetes ServiceTypes will enable greater specification of the exact type of service that you wish to retrieve. Remember that your preliminary setting is ClusterIP.

Type values, along with these values' specific behaviors, are the following:

ClusterIP: It reveals the service directly on an IP that is cluster-internal. This is significant because selecting this value will allow the service only to be accessible from inside of the cluster. Notably, ServiceType is the default.

NodePort: It reveals each Node's IP service at a port that is static. Also, a ClusterIP service that the NodePort service is designed to route to will be produced automatically. This will allow you to more easily contact the NodePort service externally from the cluster through the following request: <NodeIP>:<NodePort>.

LoadBalancer: It is responsible for exposing service in an external manner by employing a load balancer from a cloud provider. In this way, ClusterIP and NodePort are produced (the external load balancer will route to this).

ExternalName: It maps the specific service to each of the contents within the field of the externalName. It does this by returning, with its value, a CNAME record. Remember that no proxy is going to be set up in this scenario. A version of 1.7 or above of kube-dns will be needed.

The Kubernetes master is then going to automatically assign a port from a field determined through your ServiceNode; this is only in instances where you first establish the type field to NodePort. Thereafter, all of the Nodes will then proxy the port into the service that you are using- with the same port number on all of the Nodes. The port will be reported directly into your Services field.

If you wish to select certain IPs so that you can proxy your port, your nodeport-addresses kube-proxy flag should be set to specific blocks of IP. This has been supported since v1.10 Kubernetes.

To retrieve a particular port number, you are able to select a certain value in a nodePort field. Then, your chosen port is then going to be assigned to you by the system. If this path is not chosen, the API transaction will not succeed. Also, keep in mind that you are required to care for any collisions with the port on your own. Not to mention, the specific value that you select will have to be within a configured range for node ports.

Thankfully, it affords programmers their autonomy of establishing their respective load balancers and create environments not supported by Kubernetes in their entirety.

On providers of Cloud, which are responsible for supporting load balancers that are external, establishing the Type field to LoadBalancer will provide for your Service its own load balancer.

Producing the land balancer occurs in an unsynchronized manner, and all of the information therein pertaining to the balancer will be directly punished within the field. Moreover, all of the external load balances' traffic is then going to be directed to your backend Pods. The exact process in which this will operate will entirely depend upon whatever cloud provider is being used. Note that a considerable number of cloud providers do permit for loadBalancerIP to be given a specification.

For these instances, the load-balancer will be produced with the chosen loadBalancerIP. In case, however, that your loadBalancerIP isn't given a specification, another IP will be assigned to this loadBalancer (this new IP will be ephemeral). On the other hand, if the loadBalancerIP is given a certain specification, but the feature is unsupported by the cloud provider, the field will not be acknowledged.

For internal load balancing, it may be vital to direct all traffic from services existing within the same VPC that is being used. Note that this is primarily needed within a mixed environment. In contrast, within a DNS environment that is split-horizon, you will be required to utilize 2 specific services in order to route internal and external traffic toward your endpoints.

Chapter 5: Kubernetes Design Patterns

Following programming that had been object-oriented for many years, the emergence and documentation of design patterns occurred. Moreover, all of these patterns regularized and codified general problem-solving approaches to particular common programming issues that many systems faced. Furthermore, this codification process enhanced the general modernized programming due to making it much easier for programmers with less experience to create code relatively well-engineered. This then leads to the creation of reusable libraries and made codes far easier, faster, and more reliable to create.

The modern, or "state-of-the-art" with regards to distributed system engineering, has an appearance very similar to programming in the early 80s as opposed to development that is object-oriented.

Still, it's clear from viewing how successful MapReduce patterns have been with regards to bringing "Big Data" programs to the fore in many different developers and fields, that quality can be greatly improved by instilling effective patterns. Also, accessibility and speed can improve the quality as well in distributed system programming.

Nevertheless, the success that MapReduce has enjoyed is mostly limited only to. Single language for programming. Creating a fully comprehensive package of patterns for system designs will require simpler, and more generic vehicles that are language-neutral to convey all of the various atoms within the system.

As a result, it is fortunate that recent years have experienced a stark rise in Linux container technology being adopted. The container and image for the container are abstractions that are required for developing system patterns that are distributed.

Until this point, container images and containers have garnered most of their popularity through being more reliable and effective for delivering software through all of its stages, from development to production. By being continually sealed, with dependencies carries along with them, and thereby fostering deployment signals that are atomic, they will enhance the previous modern deploying software within the cloud or datacenter.

In this way, containers still carry potential to be more than merely a vehicle for deployment—they can also be similar to objects within software systems that are object-oriented.

Single-container management patterns offer a natural boundary for interface categorizing, analogous to the object boundary. Further, containers can reveal not only functionality that is application-specific, but hooks used for management systems as well. Granted, the traditional and most commonly used interface for container management is very, very limited. Generally, containers export 3 key verbs: stop, pause and run. While this interface is not entirely useless and does still have value, a richer more modernized and interface offers far greater utility to operators and developers of systems. With the broad support for HTTP web servers within most state-of-the-art programming language expansive support for many formats such as JSON, it can be relatively simple to define management API that is HTTP-based that is able to be implemented by ensuring that the container host a web server that certain end-points, along with its main function.

In this upward direction, the container is able to reveal a richer collection of information for applications, which incorporates including application-specific metrics for monitoring. Conversely, in the downward direction, the specific container interface will facilitate an environment to define and clarify lifecycles that ease writing components for software operated by management configurations and systems.

For instance, a management system for clusters will usually allocate certain priorities to particular assignments and tasks. However, tasks that are considered to be more important, or "higher priority" will be operated even in instances when clusters are oversubscribed. This is enforced by removing tasks that are less of a priority. Until resources are made available, these lower-priority tasks will have to wait.

Removing tasks of lesser priority, or evicting them, can be achieved through deleting the low-priority task. However, this will burden developers to more urgently respond to death that occurs in any area of the code.

In the instance of a lifecycle that is formal being defined

between management and application system, the components of the applications will be able to be managed much easier because they conform to a contract that is more defined. Also, the system's development will be made easier because the developer is able to rely on the contract.

To exemplify, Kubernetes employs a deletion that is "graceful." This is a Docker feature that will immediately warn a container through the SIGTERM signal that it will be terminated. This warning provides a period of time that is application-defined prior to the SIGKILL signal being sent. As a result, this allows the application to be terminated in a cleaner manner through completing operations in-flight.

An example of a lifecycle that is more complex, think about the Android Activity model; it features many callbacks as well as a more defined machine state for the way that the system will trigger callbacks. Devoid of Android lifecycles that are formal and reliable, these lifecycles would be much more difficult to formulate.

Within container-based systems, this will mainly generalize to hooks that are application-defined and triggered once a container is produced, terminated and started.

Another form of Kubernetes design patterns is multi-container and single-node application patterns. Past the single container interface, many design patterns that span containers will begin to emerge. The patterns mentioned the far are examples of this. However, single node patterns are comprised of symbiotic containers co-scheduled directly not a single host machine.

Managing containers in system support for co-scheduling a few containers as one atomic unit—this is an abstraction that Kubernetes refers to as "Pods." On the other hand, Nomad calls this, "task groups." As a result, this is a required feature if you wish to facilitate patterns.

Sidecar Patterns

This is broadly considered the most common pattern deployments for multi-containers. The role of sidecars is to improve and expand the system's main container. For instance, there may be a scenario where the main container could be a server on the web, and it may even be coupled with a "logsaver" sidecar that is responsible for collecting the web server's logs located in the local disk. Thereafter, it is streamed toward a cluster storage system.

Also, another example that occurs quite often is when a web server from disk content (local) that comes to be populated by a sidecar container. Further, this sidecar container will, once in a while, sync content from a repository and or another source of data.

Both examples presented here tend to be most common at Google. Indeed, sidecars are realized and made possible due to containers sharing a machine will also share a localized disk volume.

It is certainly possible to effectively construct the functionality of sidecars directly in the main container. Still, however, there remain several different benefits to employing separate containers.

Sidecar containers are still able to be configured in a manner that affords low-latency responses that remain consistent, especially with regard to low-latency queries. Nevertheless, this is only the case where the logsaver container is specifically configured for the purpose of scavenging extra cycles of CPU whenever the web server isn't too busy.

Also, the sidecar container is the particular unit of packaging; therefore, parting serving and log-saving into a multitude of containers will ease the division of responsibilities, thereby allowing for independent testing.

Additionally, sidecar containers are also the unit of reuse, so they can be coupled with various "main" category containers. Moreover, sidecar containers afford failure containment boundaries, thereby enabling the overall system to diminish in a relatively graceful manner.

Finally, the container is foundational the deployment unit; this allows for all of the various aspects of functionality to be improved/upgraded, as well as rolled back when it needs to be (independently). It is worth noting this benefit is accompanied by a drawback: the matrix setup for testing the system altogether needs to consider the entirety of the combinations for the container version that one may encounter in production. These can be relatively expansive because containers, on the whole, cannot be atomically upgraded.

It is granted that a monolith application will not have this same problem—still, systems that are componentized will be far easier to test in many different ways because they are constructed from smaller units that are able to be tested in an independent manner.

Ambassador Patterns

Ambassador containers are able to proxy all communication to and from main containers. For instance, a developer may choose to couple a specific application that communicates to a protocol for memcache with a twemproxy ambassador. This is due to the application assuming that it is communicating on localhost to an individual memcache.

This specific category of container pattern is useful because it simplifies a programmer's processes in 3 distinct ways:

1. Programmers will only have to consider programming with regard to their application being connected to a localhost single server.

2. This allows them to test the application on its own through running a memcache on a machine that is local rather than an ambassador.

3. Programmers are able to recycle a twemproxy ambassador along with subsequent applications that may employ different language for coding.

Adapter patterns are the final single-node pattern—as opposed to the aforementioned ambassador pattern, which is responsible for presenting applications with a clarified and simple view of different applications. This is achieved through having output and interfaces be standardized along a multitude of different containers.

An established example of adapter patterns is that adapters make sure that containers within a given system share an interface for monitoring. Currently, applications employ a broad range of methods and strategies for exporting metrics. Still, it remains much easier for single monitoring tools to gather metrics from sets of applications that are heterogeneous as long as all applications in the system are equipped with a monitoring interface that is consistent.

With regards to Google, the code convention has already been achieved. However, this is possible only when building software from the ground up. Moreover, this adapter pattern allows for heterogeneous open-source applications to create an interface that is uniform devoid of having to modify original applications.

Notably, main containers are able to "speak" with adapters by using a shared local volume or localhost. Keep in mind that although many current saluting for monitoring is capable of communicating with different types of backends, they employ codes that are application-specific within the monitoring system. As a result, this affords to separate concerns in a manner that is not as clean.

Expanding ahead of containers that are cooperating within a single machine, modular containers ameliorate constructing coordinated applications that are multi-node and distributed.

Among the biggest and predominate issues within distributed systems are leader elections. Though replication can be utilized in a way that shares load with a multitude of similar instances of components, a more intricate employment of replication are applications that require having to distinguish a "leader" from a specific replica.

Other replicas are available to replace the leader in an expedited way if they experience failure. Also, a certain system might operate a collection of leader election in a parallel manner. This may be done in order to determine the leaders of a multitude of shards. In addition, there are many different libraries for triggering a leader election. Generally, these are very complicated to fully 'understand and employ effectively. They are also inhibited by having to be used with a certain language for programming.

Alternatively, attaching a leader election and its library to an application is to employ a container for a leader election. Further, a collection of leader-election containers is capable of triggering an election on their own. They are also able to present a more simplified version of HTTP API on localhost to an application that needs a leader election.

Leader-elect containers are capable of being built only once, only by programmers who are experienced in this department. Subsequent interfaces can be recycled by developers for applications without having considered the language of implementation.

Work Queue Patterns

Work queues, in the same way as leader elections, are a thoroughly examined topic with a multitude of frameworks that implement them. Also, queues are an example of distributed systems. These patterns can retrieve architectures that are container-oriented.

The abundant availability of containers capable of implementing interfaces that mount and run allow for easier operation and implementation of a framework for queues. In this way, a developer or programmer is only required to construct containers that are capable of taking input data on filesystems and altering them to another output file. As a result, the container in this instance then becomes a stage of a work queue. For all other work that is required in formulating a work queue, this can be achieved by utilizing a simple queue capable of being reused when required.

The final Kubernetes system pattern examined in this section is the gather/scatter pattern. Within this particular system, a client that's externally operating will deliver requests initially to a "parent" or "root" node. Thereafter, the root will send the request to a broad amount of servers so that they can perform parallel computations. Partial data will be returned by each shard, and the root will then collect all of the data and deliver them into an individual response to the initial request.

Chapter 6: Kubernetes Client Libraries & Extensions

Kubernetes Client Libraries tend to operate certain tasks including authentication for users. Many client libraries are able to uncover and utilize the Kubernetes Service Account in order to authenticate whether each API client is operating within a Kubernetes cluster. On the other hand, client libraries are able to comprehend the format for the kubeconfig file in order to read all of the credentials, along with the address for the API Server.

Notably, most client libraries for Kubernetes are under the purview of Kubernetes
SIG API machinery. Not to mention, there are also client libraries that are community-maintained. Full lists of the client libraries for the Kubernetes platform can be found on their website: kubernetes.io.

In order to effectively write applications that employ Kubernetes REST API, you are not required to employ API requests and call types on your own. What's more is that you are able to employ a client library for whichever language of programming that you choose to use.

Kubernetes client libraries commonly deal with certain tasks aligned with authentication for users. Now, note that most client libraries are capable of discovering and employing a Kubernetes Service Account for authentication. However, this is only for instances when the API client is operating within a Kubernetes cluster.

One of the fascinating facets of Kubernetes is that you are able to extend the system's API if you wish to construct a platform for leveraging the full expanse of Kubernetes' power.

All of the various mechanisms that are available for employing API extensions are categorized under (CRD) Custom Resource Definition, along with an Aggregated API Server. Moreover, the APIs that use these mechanisms are each able to be accessed through Kubectl—you do not need to use a CLI if you wish to access them.

Mainly, there are 3 primary constructs that are involved in an extended Kubernetes API. These 3 components are as follows:

1. Custom sub-resource
2. Custom controller
3. Custom Kind

Custom Kind is a specific construct facilitating users to clearly define requirements that are domain-specific within a format that is declarative. For instance, a Kind for PostgreSQL that is custom is able to support a declarative model for formulating users and several databases. Indeed, a Custom Kind is analogous to native Kubernetes Kinds such as Service and Pod. Moreover, this will include status, spec, and metadata section.

Custom Controller refers to a Kubernetes controller performing reunification of cluster's state through viewing delete and update events directly onto Kubernetes Kinds within a cluster. Note that this may include native Kinds, such as Service, Pod, and Deployment - all of which were mentioned earlier in this book.

Custom Sub-facilitates uses to define actions that are relatively fine-grained on its Kind; this applies to whether the Kubernetes Kind is custom or native. Devoid of a sub-resource, Kubernetes will afford basic CRUD moves on whichever Kind is chosen. It is very important to consider that not all extended APIs will incorporate all constructs. In truth, 4 patterns have been outlined has it pertains to an extended API. These are as follows:

Custom Controller + Custom Kind. As the most well-known pattern, this affords users to utilize a Custom Kind to model one's domain equipment in a declarative manner. This will include the appropriate logic for reconciling testate of a cluster through reacting immediately to the full range of occurrences that relate to the Custom Kind. Operator Pattern is the most popular reference name for this particular pattern.

Notably, this pattern is able to be employed through Aggregated API Servers *and* CRD formats.

The formula of **Custom sub-resource + Custom Kind + Custom Controller** is the same as Operator Pattern. Moreover, it is fully capable of supporting certain custom actions that exist outside of CRUD on each Custom Kind. This is done through the custom sub-resource. If you wish to implement this specific pattern through only the Aggregated API Servers format, the **Custom sub-resource + Custom Controller** is the formula that must be used.

Granted, this will not be able to define an entirely new Kind. Instead, the logic for reconciliation is achieved by the custom controller only on events that are concerned with Kinds registered within a cluster beforehand.

Also, a custom sub-resource is utilized to access data collected by a custom controller. One of the best examples of this is an instance where a controller is responsible for maintaining and collecting data pertaining to the composition of the custom sub-resource and where Kubernetes Objects are utilized to retrieve this data. Importantly, this can only be achieved through employing the Aggregated API Servers.

In a Custom sub-resource, a custom controller is entirely absent. Moreover, this custom sub-resource is most commonly utilized as a mechanism to learn more intensive information pertaining to some facet of Kubernetes Object. The best way to exemplify this is by examining a server for metrics. Moreover, a metrics server is designed to retrieve data from Prometheus and thereafter ensures that it is made widely available through a custom sub-resource. Once again, only the Aggregated API Servers (AA) can implement this particular pattern.

It is very important to note that in every wherein an emerging Custom Kind is introduced, this pattern can be referred to an Operator Pattern. In addition, the final two patterns are primarily focused on facilitating the capability to trigger actions that are custom on Kubernetes Objects.

By analyzing all of the currently accessible examples, this section as presented 4 distinct occurrences and patterns that combine all of the constructs available today. When examining API extensions by using extension patterns, the proper mechanisms, tools, and examples are readily at your disposal when you begin formulating the extended API. Kubernetes is highly configurable and extensible. As a result, there is rarely a need to fork or submit patches to the Kubernetes project code.

Even still, there are more aspects to consider when on the subject on Kubernetes extensions. The rest of this chapter will delve deeper into these areas and present a few where the concepts are most applicable to users.

Before delving deeper into Kubernetes Extensions, Configuration is worth your consideration. Flags and files of Configuration are well docents within the section of Reference in the online documentation. Underneath each individual binary, you must consider that files and flags will not be perennially changeable within a Kubernetes service that is hosted—or even a managed distribution installation.

In instances where these are able to be changed, they can usually only be changed by cluster administrators. Not to mention, these will certainly be able to be changed in versions of Kubernetes in the near future. What's more, setting these up will most certainly require a restarting process. For this reason, users are well advised only to use these when options are limited, or if this is the only option available.

Moving back to Kubernetes extensions, it is worth being reminded that extensions are specific components of software responsible for extending and integrating on a deeper level with Kubernetes. Even more, extensions adapt to support and maintain newer forms of system hardware fully.

In most cases, cluster administrators tend to utilize a distribution and to toast instances with regard to Kubernetes. Consequently, many users of Kubernetes will be required to have extensions installed and many users will no longer be required to author brand new extensions.

Specifically designed to automate through writing particular client programs, beneficial automation can be garnered through all programs that write and or read to Kubernetes API. Moreover, there are certain patterns that can write client programs configured to operate effectively with Kubernetes that is called a Controller pattern.

When combining new APIs for Automation, users will often need also to consider adding a control loop that is capable of writing and reading new APIs in the system. When this occurs, this pattern is referred to as an Operator. Also, control loops and Custom APIs are able to be used for controlling resources which includes policies, storage, and other features as well.

When users are extending Kubernetes API through the addition of custom resources, these newly attained resources will collapse into newly formed API Groups within the platform. Interestingly, users are not able to change, alter, or even replace API groups that are already in place. Indeed, the addition of an API will not allow users to directly influence existing API behavior, such as Pods, for instance. However, users will be able to do this through API Access Extensions.

Whenever a formal request manages to reach the Kubernetes API Server, the sequence is as follows: First, it will be authenticated, followed by being Authorized. Thereafter, the steps are entirely subject to a range of versions of Admission Control. All of the steps in this process affords extensions points.

Kubernetes also has a bevy of methods for authentication that are built right into the platform. Also, it is able to be placed behind a proxy for authentication.

Another area worth examining with regard to Kubernetes Extensions are the Infrastructure Extensions. Notably, there are two key forms of Infrastructure Extensions. First, Storage Plugins: to set volume types devoid of support that is built-in, Flex Volumes are required. This happens by through having a Kubelet call directly for a Binary Plugin for effectively mounting the volume.

Next, Device Plugins: these afford nodes across the platform to find new resources for Nodes through a particular Device Plugin.

Scheduler Extensions

This is specifically a form of controller responsible for keeping close watch over pods, thereby assigning pods to nodes as well. Moreover, the scheduler default can be entirely replaced, even as still uses other components of the Kubernetes platform. Additionally, a few schedulers are able to operate simultaneously.

This is particularly significant when considering that all users of Kubernetes are not required to significantly alter the scheduler within the platform in any way whatsoever. Not to mention, the schedulers are also capable of fully supporting a webhook. This allows for a backend webhook, otherwise known as a scheduler extension, to effectively prioritize and filter all nodes that are selected for each pod.

There are myriad benefits to API Extensions within the Kubernetes platform. For instance, at the Platform layer, implementing a system will introduce all new abstractions for delivering whichever platform that the user desires. There used only to be a single avenue through which new abstractions were produced- this was through wrapping all of the APIs of the layer underneath.

Kubernetes extensions can be written as platform abstractions rather than API wrappers. Thus, this results in a few advantages:

1. Tools that are written specifically for Kubernetes base, such as Helm, are very easily utilized with certain abstractions that are uniquely produced as API extensions. However, this is likely not to be the case with regard to abstractions that are produced specifically as wrappers for API.

2. End users of Kubernetes' abstractions are not required to adopt new CLI in order to consume them fully.

3. To achieve maximum simplicity, sometimes abstractions that are produced as API wrappers can shield many of the underlying functions of API. As a result, end users are far less likely to acquire the level of control that is needed.

4. Auditing and other forms of advanced functionality that can work effectively with the base format of Kubernetes are able to very easily be leveraged for certain abstractions that are produced by only using

API extensions. However, this is likely not to be the case when considering abstractions as strictly API wrappers. Thus, users will be required to care for certain advanced functions for abstraction layers within the code.

Conclusion

Thank you again for downloading this book!

I hope this book was able to help you understand how to operate Kubernetes in its full capacity while providing in-depth information about the platform overall.

The next step is to begin implementing the strategies and practical methods presented within this text. If you are looking for new ways to use this platform or are simply trying to acquire more information about Kubernetes, this is the perfect text for you!

Given the abundance of information available on the Internet pertaining to best practices of digital platforms, there has yet to be any extensive text on the Kubernetes platform. With 6 chapters that present and elaborate on the multiple features of Kubernetes, you are now fully equipped to maximize this platform for everything that it is.

Be sure to study all of the examples presented to ensure the smoothest operation and navigation of the platform. This will save you time and energy while making sure that you get the most out of your projects.

Finally, if you enjoyed this book, then I'd like to ask you for a favor: would you be kind enough to leave a review for this book on Amazon? It'd be greatly appreciated!

Thank you and good luck!

Docker

A Step-by-Step Guide to Learn and Master Docker

Introduction

Innovation in today's fast-paced and interconnected society comes directly from the software. Developers need to be able to provide an intuitive, attractive, and easily accessible experience for their users in order to succeed. Docker's modern platform can provide that kind of innovation to all of its users with its unique method of packaging up applications into isolated, independent, and contained environments in order to maximize their portability as well as their efficiency. Docker has been referred to as "The modern platform for high-velocity innovation," and is currently the only independent container platform that can allow you to build, share, and even run any application easily and efficiently from anywhere you choose.

I would like to thank you for purchasing and downloading this copy of "Docker: A Step by Step Guide to Learn and Master Docker." I would also like to offer you a short word of congratulations for taking the first steps on the way to learning about, and mastering one of the world's most efficient and versatile platforms that can allow you to easily and seamlessly develop, ship, and run any application from anywhere you want. Of course, this refers to the Docker platform, which uses completely unique technology, referred to as the "container" to give Docker's users the ability to quickly and easily package up an application in a "contained" environment. These containers and the isolation that they provide can also allow for extra security in your application as well as the ability to run multiple containers at the same time without affecting performance.

Of course, there is a little bit more to the Docker platform than simply this "innovation." Docker is a unique platform for a tool that can be called nothing short of a "game-changer." Such a unique and innovative service like Docker and all of its various products and services will also inherently require a much higher amount of learning and adjustment in order to understand and master when compared to other similar services. There can be a bit of a "learning curve" with new and complicated services like this one, and approaching it can even seem a little bit intimidating at first.

This is why this book exists! This step by step guide to learning and mastering Docker is meant to help you do exactly what it says on the cover; learn and master Docker. This incredibly helpful book is meant to serve as your guide in understanding many of the various different products and services that Docker offers to its users, as well as a number of the different features that exist within those products and services and how to use them as effectively as possible in order to maximize the benefits of using this incredibly unique service. Additionally, this book will go over all of the little ins and outs of the Docker platform and its various products and services, including some tips, tricks, and shortcuts to help you even further in this goal.

This book will go over a number of different topics to give you all of the tools necessary to gain a complete understanding and mastery over Docker's various products and services. These topics include things like the various reasons why you would (and should) choose Docker over any other possibly similar service as well as some short introductions and guides to many of the various products and services that docker offers to its users such as Docker Enterprise and Docker Desktop for Mac or Windows, and the Docker Hub. This book will also go over many of the different features of Docker's various products and services, as well as how to actually use them at a fundamental level in order to help you to master this incredibly innovative platform for building and running applications as smoothly and efficiently as possible.

Chapter 1: Introduction to Docker

Docker can be a very useful tool for developers and system administrators, and can allow for much the much easier deployment of various applications by allowing its user to pack up those applications and their necessary resources into tidy and easy to access packages, which are referred to as "containers." Docker is described by Wikipedia as an open-source project that automates the deployment of software applications inside containers by providing an additional layer of abstraction and automation of OS-level virtualization on Linux. In simpler terms that will be easy to understand, this means that Docker is a tool that is meant to allow developers and system administrators to be able to deploy their applications within a discrete container that will allow that application to run much more easily and efficiently on a particular system. The primary benefit that docker is able to provide to its users is to box up (or contain) an application with all of the resources that it needs in order to function properly into one compact unit that is meant for software development. This is an incredibly innovative tool that is designed to help make it much easier for developers to build and run different applications on any system by using these containers. Containers can help in doing this by ensuring that an application will be able to run efficiently and easily by allowing developers to store their applications and all of their various part such as the libraries and other resources than the application needs in order to run properly into a container. By doing this, you will be able to make sure that all of your applications will be able to run the same way regardless of the system that they are being used on.

Docker is developed with the primary intention of being used for the Linux operating system. It uses a number of different useful features of the Linux kernel, such as kernel namespaces and cgroups, as well as a union compatible filing system that can allow for several independent containers to be run within a single instance of Linux. This can be very helpful in avoiding the overhead that can be experienced in starting up and maintaining a virtual machine. The support for namespaces within Linux can serve to isolate an application's scope of the operating environment. This includes things like mounted file systems, different networks, process trees, and user IDs. Additionally, the cgroups of the Linux kernel can provide resource limiting for the CPU and the memory of the system. As of version 0.9, Docker has also included a feature called the libcontainer library, which functions as docker's own methods of directly using various virtualization features that are provided by the Linux kernel, as well as using various abstracted interfaces designed for the purpose of virtualization. For these reasons, docker is used primarily by developers and system administrators and is designed with this in mind. For a developer, this means that you can focus solely on writing the code for your applications without needing to worry about its compatibility with a different system that it might be run on. It will also allow you to get a bit of a jump ahead by using one of several thousands of programs that are already designed to be run within a docker container as part of your own application. Docker can help to provide flexibility to developers and to system administrators in this way, and can greatly reduce the number of systems that are needed, due to its low overhead and smaller footprint.

Docker is, in some ways, similar to a virtual machine. However, it does also differ from virtual machines in that rather than trying to create an entire virtual operating system, docker will instead simply allow an application to use the same Linux kernel that the system it is being run on uses, and only requires that an application is shipped with the resources that it requires to run that are not already provided on the host system. This can allow the application to run much more efficiently and with a very significant boost to performance. It can also drastically reduce the application's overall size, too. Additionally, docker is completely open-source. This means that anyone can alter and contribute to docker in order to improve it or tailor it to meet their own specific needs if they require extra features that are not included by default. Docker is separated from virtual machines by its ability to utilize the resources that are already provided by the Linux kernel (especially with namespaces and cgroups) which can allow it to function without a separate operating system. Instead of a separate simulated operating system, like a virtual machine, a Docker container is able to build on to the kernel's functionality.

Containers can be somewhat difficult to understand, however. The basic idea of these containers was discussed briefly earlier in this chapter, but they should also probably be explained in more detail, as these containers will be the basis for most of the information to be contained in this book. A container can be described as a tight, discrete package that is designed to contain an application and all of the files that it needs to run in an efficient way that can allow them to stay isolated from the system that they are being run and hosted on. Containers have become more and more popular recently, as they can help to offer a much more logical packaging mechanism by allowing for specific applications to be run separately and independently from the system that they are being "hosted" by. This separation can allow container-based applications to maintain consistency easily and regardless of their current host system. This can include a wide variety of various environments, such as a public cloud, private data centers, or even the personal laptop computer of a developer of the application. This can give a developer the ability to build and test their applications in predictable, consistent environments that are isolated and controlled, which can allow for much more versatility, allowing the application to be run from anywhere.

Virtual machines have become the industry standard used to build and run software applications. Virtual machines run applications within another guest operating system, which is dependent on virtual simulation of the operating system, which is powered and maintained by the server's host operating system. A virtual machine can be very useful for providing complete isolation of various processes for applications in a number of different ways. For example, there are very few ways in which an issue in the host system's operating system is able to affect the software that is being run within the guest operating system and vice versa. However, this does come with a very high cost. There is also a very large amount of "overhead," which in this case refs to computational power that is effectively wasted and that is spent during the processes of starting up and maintaining the Virtual Machine, in order to simulate the host's hardware for a guest operating system.

Containers, on the other hand, have a slightly different method of approaching this task. A container can provide a large majority of the necessary isolation for these processes that a virtual machine can provide with much less overhead, using significantly lowered amounts of computing power than virtual machines, by using the much simpler mechanics of the host's operating system as opposed to virtually recreating the whole operating system.

Because of these unique benefits, containers (as well as docker, by extension) have been seeing widespread success. Large companies such as Facebook, Google, and Netflix have taken to using containers in order to help make large teams of engineers even more productive and to help in improving the efficiency at which those teams are able to utilize computational resources. Google has even credited the elimination of the need to possess and maintain large data centers to their adoption and use of containers.

Additionally, a lot of the technologies that power Docker's containers are completely open-source. This means that there is a large community made up of various contributors who all help to develop the products and a large number of similar or related projects that fit the needs of many different kinds of organization and groups. Arguably one of the most significant reasons for many people's recently sparked interest in this new container-based technology has been docker's "open source project" which is a command-line tool that has made creating and using containers much easier for developers as well as system administrators. Container technology has generated large amounts in interest in "microservice architecture," which is a specific method of designing and developing applications that involved breaking down more complex applications into several much smaller, more flexible portions that can easily work together. Each part of these applications is designed and developed independently, with the application as a whole being made up of all of these smaller pieces combined. Each of these pieces can be placed within a container and scaled separately from the rest of the larger, complete application.

Chapter 2: Why should you Choose Docker?

Based on the recent success of container technology, there are a number of reasons to utilize this incredibly useful and innovative tool. Docker has become the leader in the market of container technology by combining its container platform with a number of incredibly helpful services in order to help give developers all of the freedom that they require in order to effectively and efficiently build and maintain their applications without having to worry about becoming "locked-in" with a specific industry-standard technology. Many modern businesses have experienced a sense of pressure to transform their companies, but are limited by these kinds of applications and technologies that prevent them from doing so. Docker can help to remedy this issue by allowing these companies to "unlock their potential," giving them much more freedom and the means to develop their products with a container platform that can introduce their traditional applications and services to an automated, secure supply chain and allow them to improve collaboration within their companies.

Within modern companies, innovation is heavily reliant on powerful and effective software. Organizations that succeed in the modern marketplace are able to do so by becoming more software-oriented and by empowering their software developers to efficiently and effectively create new and engaging experiences for their customers. Naturally, these experiences will usually take the form of various applications that can run on a variety of different systems. Docker can allow a company to achieve all of these goals by giving them the best experience in developing useful applications that will allow for higher levels of success and cooperation within the company. In addition to allowing for much more ease in building useful and intuitive applications, the Docker platform also provides scaled security features that can continue to function without slowing the process of development. This is because of the fact that the docker platform has been built upon various industry-standard technologies with open source software such as Docker and Kubernetes. This platform is used by millions of individuals and companies around the world. Docker also includes a completely unrivaled library of content that is built for use with containers, which contains upward of 100,000 separate container images from various sources within the docker development community.

Docker has a number of incredibly useful and varied features. It can function efficiently with any programming, application framework, and even operating system. Docker can provide developers with the freedom to select the best tools for them and their uses, as well as various programming languages and appropriate application frameworks for any project that they might be working on. Docker Enterprise is one of the only container platforms that can give you complete freedom of the operating system and infrastructure that you use. Docker can provide this type of excellence in a number of different areas. It has a number of useful features that can help developers to create applications that are efficient and easy to use while also streamlining the development processes for these applications. These features include various capabilities such as automated application scanning and signing for the purpose of policy enforcement, multi-layered security features, and the ability to build and deploy portable and secure hybrid cloud applications without getting in the way of the productivity of app development. There are a number of specific features that docker provides and various reasons why you should use Docker. These reasons will be detailed below:

Cost-effectiveness and returns on investments. One significant advantage of choosing to use Docker is the return on investment. This is one of the most significant motivations behind a lot of management decisions, especially those regarding the selection of new products. The more a specific solution can reduce costs and overhead while also raising the profits of a company, the better this solution will prove to be. This applies especially to large companies that have already been established in their market and need to maintain a more long term source of steady revenue. In this way, docker can help to save developers money by drastically reducing their overhead in terms of both financial costs and infrastructure resources. Docker can allow for the need for much fewer resources of this type in order to develop and run various applications. Because of these reduced overhead costs, docker can allow businesses and other types of companies to save on every aspect of their operations from the cost of maintaining servers to the employees that are actually needed in order to do so. Docker allows teams of engineers to be much smaller, and much more effective, enabling companies to maximize their efficiency and effectiveness.

Increased productivity. Docker containers can allow for higher levels of consistency in development and the standardization of the environment. This type of standardization is actually one of the most significant advantages of using a docker based architecture system.

Docker can provide repeatable building, production, and testing environments as well. Being able to completely standardize the service infrastructures for all of the various parts of the operation can allow every member of a team to work more efficiently with each other and to communicate more easily with each other about various parts of the whole. By doing this, the team will be much more well equipped to efficiently find, analyze, and resolve any issues that exist in the application. This can help to increase efficiency and productivity for the team as well.

Container image efficiency. Docker can allow you to build a single container image and then use that image across all of the steps of the deployment process. This will allow you also to separate independent steps and to run them in parallel to each other. This can speed up the build to the production process by large amounts of time.

Compatibility. Docker allows you to eliminate the issue of compatibility for good. One of the largest and most significant benefits that docker can provide is "parity." With regards to docker, this means that all of your applications and images will be able to run the same way regardless of the device they are being used on. For a developer, this can make it much easier to actually develop their apps by spending much less time preparing environments for their applications. This will also make it much easier for you to maintain a stable production infrastructure at a basic level simply.

Simplicity! Another incredibly huge benefit that docker can provide is simplicity to its users. Users are able to use their own configuration without any issues. As docker is able to be used in a large number of environments, the infrastructure's requirements are no longer connected to the application's environment.

Quick and efficient deployment. Docker is a unique service in that it is able to reduce the time that it takes for deployment down to a matter of seconds. This incredibly fast deployment time is a result of Docker's unique container-based platform. Docker will create a container for each individual process that needs to be carried out, as opposed to booting an OS for those processes. This can also allow for quicker and easier creation and destruction of specific portions of information without having to worry about the processing power that is needed to bring it up again, becoming higher than can be allowed.

Continuous testing and deployment. Docker containers are configured by default to automatically maintain all of its dependencies and settings internally, in order to ensure environments that are as consistent as is possible at all stages of development. This allows Docker's users to be able to use the same containers while guaranteeing that there are no inconsistencies or unexpected variables during every step of development and production. However, if you ever need to make any sort of changes to a product during its release cycle, this can also be done quickly and easily. You can easily make any necessary changes to your containers and then test and implement any of those changes as well. The flexibility of Docker's containers is one of the most significant advantages of using this software, along with the other benefits that Docker can provide to its users.

Multi-cloud platforms. This is arguably one of the most significant reasons to choose docker over other options. Over time, there has been a very clear trend of major cloud computing service providers, such as amazon web services (AWS) and the Google Compute Platform (GCP) beginning to acknowledge and recognise the unrivaled availability and utility that Docker and its various services can provide to their users. Docker containers are able to be run inside of a wide variety of different platforms such as the Google Compute Engine, VirtualBox, and many others as well, as long as the host system's operating system is able to support Docker. Additionally, docker containers that are being run within one environment like an Amazon EC2 instance are able to quickly and easily be ported to other environments as well. Even if a container is ported to a new environment in this way, it will still maintain the same or similar consistency and functionality as the original environment, which can allow for a much smoother experience for developers and system administrators.

Isolation. Another very useful and attractive feature that docker can provide to its users is the isolation and segregation of all of your applications and resources. Docker ensures that every container has all of its own resources that are necessary for it to function and that those resources are completely isolated from those of other containers. You can even run multiple different containers for their own separate applications on completely separate stacks. Docker can help you by ensuring the clean and efficient removal of any application if this is necessary because all of your container-based applications are able to be run on their own separate containers. If you find that you do not need a particular application anymore, you can simply delete its container to remove it from your machine, and there will not be any files that are leftover from that application hiding within your host operating system. Additionally, docker can also make sure that each of its container-based applications is only allowed to use the resources that have already been assigned to those applications. Usually, a particularly "heavy" application might take up a lot of resources and cause a drop in the quality of performance or even downtime, but this is not a concern for container-based applications.

Security. The final benefit that will be listed here is another very important one. Again, docker can make sure that all of the applications that are running on containers are entirely separate and remain isolated from other applications and from the files on your host operating system. This allows Docker's users to maintain absolute control over the flow of traffic on the host, as well. A Docker container is never able to view any information about the files or processes that are running inside another container.

Chapter 3: Docker Products and Services

The Docker platform offers a number of separate integrated products and services that can be used to help you to build, run, and even share your container-based applications from your own system to the cloud. This is possible because the Docker platform has been based on the core building blocks of the docker brand and various tools that have come from Docker such as Docker Desktop, Docker Engine, and Docker Hub. Docker provides a number of incredibly useful tools that can help you to build, run, and share applications. Docker's desktop tools for developers can help you to streamline the process of delivering new container-based apps and tools and to make it easier and simpler to store applications that you have already build in containers moving forward. You will be able to run applications that are based on containers and manage those containers with services like the enterprise platform. You can even utilize tools like the docker container image library, docker hub, in order to accelerate your innovation. Docker hub can help you to explore millions of container images that have been made available by verified publishers within the community. As was stated previously, docker provides a large number of different services to help you in developing and distributing applications, which will all be described in more detail within this chapter.

Docker enterprise. This is one of Docker's biggest products. Docker Enterprise is the largest platform for applications that are based on container technology and allows you to build, share, and run all of your applications easily. Docker Enterprise can provide a secure supply chain for software and can deploy a wide range of applications to maximize its potential as well as your own. It can help in the automation of a number of tasks such as the provisioning of various containers, pods, and resources. Docker Enterprise also includes the docker universal control plane. This is Docker's own cluster management solution which can be installed onto your own system or in your private cloud and can help you to manage all of your applications and clusters from one place.

Docker Hub is another one of the incredibly useful tools that Docker provides to its users. Docker's Hub is a sort of common storage space meant to help developers share their own container files with others. The hub has a number of different developers and independent software creators that help to contribute content to it with their own container images from various open-source projects. Docker Hub's users can gain access to an unparalleled number of free public repositories of container images that other developers within the community have previously stored. With a paid subscription plan, Docker Hub's users can also gain access to its private repository feature, as well.

Docker also provides to its users a number of useful technologies. The first one to note is Docker's developer tools. These can help to improve developers to ship their applications much faster and make it much easier to build and run effective and useful container-based applications by extending the usefulness of the Docker Engine even further.

There is also a version of Docker that has been designed for Windows and macOS machines, called Docker Desktop. Docker Desktop is meant to run on the Windows 10 operating system, and cal allows windows users to do all of the things that Docker is designed to do for Linux users. This can allow developers to build applications for Linux as well as windows, and to share them easily. Docker Desktop is by far the easiest and most effective tool for building container applications for Swarm and Kubernetes with any framework or any language.

Docker also provides an open-source system for the automated management, routing, scaling, and placement of different containers, called Kubernetes. The Docker platform contains a secure kubernetes environment that is meant for developers of many different levels of skill. This can allow for the flexibility that is necessary for experienced users while also providing ease and convenience for newer users. The docker platform can also allow teams and individuals alike to run kubernetes interchangeably with swarm technology. This can provide a higher capacity for flexibility for users of the best tool for managing and using container-based applications.

Docker image registries can also allow you to securely store and manage your container images with your own personal registries. This is a feature that is included with the Docker Enterprise product and functions as a private image storage space for any container images that you wish to use it for. These registries can allow you to quickly and easily retrieve and build on to already existing container images. You can also create your own images yourself, as well, and then place them into your own repositories and share them with other individuals within your team or anyone else who you might wish to share them with. Security features that have been built in can also enable you and other people within your team to check on the source and the content within a container image, alongside a number of automatic functions and integration with CI/CD tools that can serve to speed up the testing and delivery of different applications.

Chapter 4: Docker Toolbox

This chapter will be about another incredibly useful feature that docker offers to its users, Docker Toolbox. The Docker Toolbox is by far the quickest way for you to get set up with Docker and begin developing your own applications. This toolbox can supply you with all of the various tools that you will need in order to get started with Docker. These tools include things like the Docker Client, Docker Machine, Docker Compose, Kitematic, and the Docker quickstart terminal app. Docker Toolbox is officially considered to be a legacy product and is meant for older Mac and Windows computers that do not meet all of the requirements for the current Mac and Windows desktop applications. If you are able to use the current Docker products, it is recommended that you do so. However, while docker Toolbox is a legacy product, Kitematic is still supported and is available for download as a separate product as well.

Docker Toolbox's various included products can cover a wide range of functions and will help you to get started as easy as possible. The Docker Machine and Virtualbox will allow you to run containers within a Linux virtual machine, which is maintained by the virtual box hypervisor. Kitematic is also a legacy product and comes bundled with the Docker toolbox. It is, of course, available to download on its own as well, however. Kitematic is an open-source solution that is meant to make the use of Docker on a Mac or a Windows PC much easier and more streamlined. Kitematic does this by automating the installation and setup process of Docker as well as providing an intuitive and simple graphical user interface to help you to run docker containers. It also works with Docker machine in order to supply a virtual machine and to install the docker engine to your system. The Kitematic user interface can supply you with various container images that you can then run right away. You are also able to use the search bar provided by Kitematic to search for specific container images that are available to the community. Or you can also use Kitematic's interface to help you to create and manage your container images quickly and easily. You can even switch back and forth between the Docker CLI and Kitematic's user interface if you want to do so. Kitematic can automate even advanced features such as volume configuration and port management.

In order to download and install Kitematic if you have not already, you can do so in a few ways. The first method of downloading and installing Kitematic is with Docker

Toolbox. As was stated earlier in this chapter, kinematic is included with the Docker Toolbox application. Of course, Docker Toolbox is intended for older systems that do not meet the requirements of any of the current products, and if you are able to, you should use these versions of Docker instead. If you are using the current Docker Desktop applications for Mac or for Windows, you can choose Kitematic from the menus within those applications, which will then start the installation process of Kitematic. You also have the option of downloading Kitematic directly from the Kitematic releases page.

Once you have installed Kitematic, you can start the application. On Desktop systems, this means clicking on the app icon. You will then be asked to log in with your Docker ID and user name. You also have the option to skip this step for now, and to browse Docker Hub as a guest, however. Once you have entered the application, you can then run applications through it. You can also find a list of all running and stopped containers on the left side of the application interface, underneath the link called "New Container." This list includes all of the containers, including ones that were not started through Kitematic, which can give you a quick and easy way to view and manage your containers. From there, you can view the logs from any container by clicking on that container. You can also restart or stop that container as well.

Docker Hub also has a page called "New Container," which allows you to search for new container images within the docker Hub to select. When you have found the specific image that you are looking for, you can run it by clicking the "create" option in order to pull that from the hub and run it.

If you select a container that is paused or stopped you can also restart or stop that container. Additionally, you will be able to view the container's output logs, and you can make any changes that you wish to make in the settings section, which will then be applied to the container if you restart it. You can also view all of the container's log outputs by clicking on the "Logs" preview or the "logs" tab. Once you have opened the logs, you can scroll through them and edit the logs as you wish. Any changes made will be applied upon restart.

Chapter 5: Public Repositories

This chapter is about Docker Hub. This topic has been talked about briefly in previous chapters, as well, but will be discussed in more detail in this chapter as well. Docker hub is the largest repository around the world of unique container images from a wide variety of sources, including various developers within the community and independent vendors for containers. Docker Hub users can gain access to all of the public repositories within the community for free and can choose a paid subscription to gain access to private repositories as well. Docker Hub's repositories are meant to allow you to share your own container images with customers, team members, or the docker community as a whole.

You can move container images to the Hub with the "Docker Push" command, and place them in a repository that way. Additionally, multiple images are able to be stored within a single repository as well. Multiple images can be added to a repository if you simply add a tag that is specific to that repository. Once you have done this, you will also be able to use the "Docker Push" command to push that repository to the appropriate registry for its name or tags. In order to "push" a repository If you want to create your own repositories, you first need to sign in to Docker Hub. Once you have signed if, you can click on the "Repositories" option, and then click on "Create Repo." When you are making a new repository, you have the option of putting it in your own Docker ID namespace or any other namespace that you are an "owner" of. When creating a repository, it is also important to note that the name of a repository does have to be unique within its namespace. Repository names can contain a minimum of 2 characters and a maximum of 255, and they can contain only lowercase letters, numbers hyphens, and underscores. The "short description" of a repository is what will be used for the purpose of search results, and will contain the first 100 characters of the "full description," which will function as the repository's "ReadMe." Once you have created a repository and titled it, you will be able to place container images into the repository with the "Docker Push" command. The images you've moved to the Hub will then be uploaded and made available to the community.

If you have access to private repositories, however, you will also be able to make your container images private, restricting them to people who have been granted access, which can either be your own account only or any account within a specific group. In order to create a private repository, you can simply select the "private" option when you are creating the repository. You can also change the settings of a repository that has already been created in order to make it private by going into its settings tab. You gain access to one private repository with your Docker Hub free account, as well, however, this free private repository will not be available to anyone but yourself. If you want to create more private repositories to share with other people you can upgrade your account with a paid Docker Hub subscription plan from the "Billing Information" page.

Once your private repository has been created, you will then be able to move your container image files to and from the repository. It is important to note that you will need to be signed in to an account that has access to a private repository in order to work with it. Additionally, private repositories can not currently be searched for through Docker's search tools. However, you are able to allow certain people or groups of people access to these private repositories, and manage their access to that repository from its settings page. You will also be able to change a repository's status between public and private if you so choose, at any time, provided you have an available slot open at that time.

A collaborator, in this context, refers to another individual who you can share access to your own private repositories with. Once you have designated a collaborator and given them access to your private repositories, they will then be able to push and pull to and from those private repositories. However, they will not be able to delete the repository or change its status from private to public, nor will they be able to perform any other sort of administrative task within those repositories, such as adding additional collaborators or restricting access from existing ones. You will also, as the owner, have the ability to change the level of the permissions to your collaborators on Docker Hub by using organizations and teams to separate certain groups of people into categories and distinct groups.

You can also view the Docker Hub's repository "Tage" in order to see all of the tags that are available as well as the size of the image that is associated with each tag. The size of an image is an expression of all of the space that is taken up by a particular image as well as each of that image's "parent" images. The image size is also a representation of the disk space that all of the contents of the image's .tar file will take up when you save that image. In order to edit the tags of a particular repository, you simply need to click on the "Manage Repository" option or find that specific repository under "Repositories." You can search within the

Docker Hub's registry with the search bar included in the Hub's interface, or by using the command line to search. When you search the Docker Hub registry in either of these ways, you will be able to locate specific images based on the name of the image, the name of the user who created the image, or the description of the image. Once you have located the image that you are searching for, you are able to then download that image with the command "docker pull <image name>:." You can also use the "star" feature of Docker Hub to mark specific images to return to at a later time. Your own images can be starred by other people, as well. The "star" feature is simply a quick and easy way to "bookmark" images that you particularly like or that you would like to revisit at a later time.

Chapter 6: Private Registries

The previous chapter of this book went over the topic of public repositories. While somewhat similar to that concept, this chapter's topic, which will be referred to as the "private registry." Docker Registry is another of the incredibly useful products that Docker provides to its users. This enterprise-grade solution is meant for the storage of various docker container images. In simple terms, Docker Registry is a service that can help you to easily and efficiently store your Container images and can be incredibly helpful for storing these images especially if you might not want your container images to be available to anyone else within the community, like with repositories stored on the Docker Hub. Private registries can be incredibly useful if you want to be able to easily manage the place where you store all of your container images. Docker Registry is also completely open-source, as well, in case you might want to alter it or add on to the application in any way.

The Docker Registry is compatible with version 1.6.0 or newer versions of the Docker engine, but Docker recommends that users who want a simpler solution that is "ready to go" and doesn't require any maintenance should instead try the Docker Hub, which can supply its users with a free hosted registry with many useful features and the option for more useful features that come with a paid subscription. The strengths and uses of the Docker Hub were discussed in the previous chapter in more depth, as well.

The Docker registry's storage is confined to drivers. The storage driver that the registry uses by default is in the local POSIX file system, in order to best suit development. However, many other cloud-based storage drivers can also be used. Developers who intend to use other storage locations can even write their own drivers. Additionally, the Docker Registry puts a very strong focus on your ability to secure access to your container images and also supports basic authentication and TLS as well. More information regarding advanced authorization and authentication methods can be found within the Docker Registry's GitHub repository.

The next topic that will be important to understand with regards to the Docker Registry is image naming. The names of various container images are used in many different docker commands. For example, the command "Docker pull ubuntu" will tell docker to "pull," or retrieve an image called "ubuntu" from the Docker Hub. This can serve as an incredibly handy shortcut for another much more lengthy command, "pull docker.io/library/ubuntu." Another very useful example of this is the "docker pull myregistrydomain:port/foo/bar" command. This can tell docker to find a registry within the location " myregistrydomain:port" in order to find and pull a specific image called "foo/bar." These are just a couple of the many different docker commands that deal directly with various images. You can also find more and learn more about many more of the different docker commands of this type in the Docker Engine's official documentation page.

Being able to run your own private registries is very easy and can complement your own continuous integration or continuous delivery systems, as well. In a normal type of workflow, any changes that are made to the source revision control system would also automatically prompt a build to be made on to your CI system as well, which would then push the new image to your docker registry, provided the build was not interrupted or prevented in some way. Once this has been completed, the registry would then be notified and would then prompt a deployment to be made for other systems also to be notified that a new container image has been made available in the registry. This is very useful for situations when you may want to deploy a new container image to a number of different machines. This is also the most effective and efficient method available to help you easily distribute a specific container image within an isolated network.

In order to use these private registries, it is recommended that you already have a familiarity with Docker. Specifically, you should be familiar with the processes of pushing and pulling docker container images. You will need to recognize the various differences between the cli and daemon as well and have a functional understanding of the basics of networking as well. While simply creating a docker private registry can be fairly easy to accomplish, being able to operate it as well will require a few additional skills, as is usually the case with most things. It is also strongly recommended that you have a familiarity with the concepts and basics of logging, log processing, systems availability and scalability, systems monitoring, and security technologies and a decent grasp of HTTP and general network communications, as well. Having a good handle on these and other similar skills can make it much easier for you to learn and understand, and even master, the various different features of Docker's private registries and how to use them.

Chapter 7: Linking Containers

This chapter will go over the concept and process of linking containers. It will also contain information about various topics related to the linking of containers, as well, such as the process of connecting with a network port and how to actually link containers. It will be very important for you to note during this chapter, however, that the link flag is considered to be a legacy feature of Docker. For Docker's users, this essentially means that the link flag feature may eventually be removed in the future. Unless for whatever reason, you have no other option than to continue to use this feature, it is strongly advised that you instead choose to use user-defined networks to help you to communicate between multiple different containers as opposed to using the link feature. It is recognized that there are features that the link feature is able to do that user-defined networks may not be able to, such as the sharing of environment variables between containers. While user defines networks do not possess this capability, there are several workarounds and other mechanisms that can be used in its place, such as using volumes to share various types of information between multiple containers. Before the

Docker networks feature was released, Docker Links could be used to allow easy and effective communication and secure data transfers between different containers. With the addition of the Docker Networks feature to Docker's impressive list of products and services, users are still able to create links between containers, but they function in slightly different ways between the default bridge network and user-defined ones.

As has been mentioned in earlier chapters of this book, each container that you create needs to have a name in order to finalize its creation, and will automatically assign a name to each container by default. You can also rename a container to something else if you want to do so. This can be done if you use the "name" flag, and you will also have the option to return the container's name with docker inspect. It is important to remember that each container's name must be unique. This means that two containers can not share the same name. This can be important to remember when assigning new names to your containers. If you want to use a name for a container that is already assigned to another one, you have first to delete the original container or assign it a new name before you can assign that name to the new container.

Docker uses the names of these containers for all tasks related to the sorting and organization of your containers. This included the establishment of links between these different containers. These names can help to organize your containers for both docker and yourself. Of course, the names of different containers can be useful to you to help you to remember which containers are which and the purposes that they serve. Additionally, Docker can also use the names of all of your different containers to identify and organize all of your containers, and it uses these names as reference points when creating links as well.

Links between containers can enable these containers to easily find each other in order to transfer data from one container to the other. By creating these links between different containers, you create a path for information to travel on from the first container, which serves as the source, to the second, which is called the recipient. This is a one-way path that allows the recipient to gain access to specific information from the source container. In order to actually create a link from one container to another, you simply need to use the "link" flag.

The first step that you will need to take in order to do this is to create a new container that contains a database. This can be done by creating your new container from the training/Postgres container image, which will then contain within it a PostgreSQL database. Once this step has been completed, you can create a new container to link to the first one with the database. "$ docker run -d -P --name [new container name] --link [name of database container]:[alias]/webapp python app.py" will allow you to link this new container to the first container with the database. The bracketed spaces should, of course, be replaced with the appropriate names where the new container is the recipient container, and the database container name and alias will represent the name and alias of the original "source" container. Once this has been completed, and your two containers have been successfully linked, you can inspect these two containers with Docker Inspect. When you do this, you should be able to see that the two containers are now linked, with the recipient container being able to retrieve information from the source. The recipient container will now be able to access various information about and from the source container and its database.

Chapter 8: Docker Commands

The next important thing that you will want to understand when you are learning about Docker and all of its various features are the commands. This chapter will be discussing the docker commands and how actually to use them effectively. This will be a very important aspect of mastering docker and getting use out of it. Depending on how your docker system is configured, it is possible that you might have to preface each of your docker commands with sudo. If you are not familiar with sudo, it stands for "substitute user do" or "super user do." Sudo can be incredibly helpful and even critical to some Linux distributions and can be useful when you are attempting to run administrative applications. In simple terms, sudo can allow one user to run a program as another user, which is most often the root user. If you want to avoid the need to use sudo with the docker command, then you (or the system administrator) will need to create a "docker" unix group and then add users to that group. Otherwise, you will need to rely on "sudo" with your docker commands.

The next things that will need to be discussed in this chapter are the configuration files. The Docker command line will typically store all of its configuration files within a directory that is named .docker, that exists within your home directory by default. You are able, however, to change this and specify a new location for these files to go to with the "DOCKER_CONFIG" environment variable. You also have the option to use the "-config" command-line option, but it will be important to note that if you use both of these methods, then the "-config" option will take priority over "DOCKER_CONFIG" and will override any settings made by using that method. Additionally, Docker uses the configuration directory and will automatically store and manage the files in this directory itself. As such, it is strongly advised that you do not modify any of these files. You can, however, safely change or modify the file called "config.json" in order to change or alter the specific ways in which the docker command will act. Docker users have the ability to change or alter the docker command behavior by using various command-line options and environment variables. Users are also able to alter various options in the config.json file to change many of the same behaviors. When you are changing and modifying these behaviors, it can be very important to consider the order of priority among these various mechanisms. For example, any command-line options that are used will automatically take priority over any environment variables that are used, and these environment variables will be prioritized over any properties that are specified in a "config.json" file. There are a number of various properties that are stored within the config.json file, which will be listed below:

HttpHeaders: The "HttpHeaders" property specifies a collection of different headers that will be included within any an all of the messages that may be sent from the Docker client to the daemon. The daemon will be discussed in the chapter on the Docker engine. In simple terms, the daemon is able to accept docker API requests and communicate with other daemons in order to manage a number of different services. Docker is not able to interpret any of these headers, and it also cannot allow these headers to affect any headers that it sets for itself. They are simply put into all of the messages that they are applied to without any effect on any other headers that docker has set for itself.

psFormat: The "psFormat" property will specify the format that is used by default for the docker ps output. If the docker ps command is used and the "--format" flag is not provided, the Docker client will automatically refer to the psFormat property for this purpose. If the psFormat property has not been set, then the docker client will then refer to the default table format, instead.

imagesFormat: The "imagesFormat" property will specify the format that is used by default for the purpose of docker images output. If the docker images command is used and the "--format" flag is not provided with it, the docker client will automatically refer to the imagesFormat property for this purpose. If the imagesFormat property has not been set, then the docker client will then refer instead to the default table format for this purpose.

pluginsFormat: The "pluginsFormat" property will specify the format that is used by default for the purpose of docker plugin ls output. If the docker plugin ls command is used and the "--format" flag is not provided with it, the docker client will automatically refer to the pluginsFormat property for this purpose. If the pluginsFormat property has not been set, then the docker client will then refer instead to the default table format for this purpose.

servicesFormat: The "servicesFormat" property will specify the format that is used by default for the purpose of docker service ls output. If the docker service ls command is used and the "--format" flag is not provided with it, the docker client will automatically refer to the serviceFormat property for this purpose. If the servicesFormat property has not been set, then the docker client will then refer instead to the default table format for this purpose.

serviceInspectFormat: The "serviceInspectFormat" property will specify the format that is used by default for the purpose of docker service inspect the output. If the docker service inspects command is used, and the "--format" flag is not provided with it, the docker client will automatically refer to the serviceInspectFormat property for this purpose. If the servicesFormat property has not been set, then the docker client will then refer instead to the default json format for this purpose.

statsFormat: The "servicesFormat" property will specify the format that is used by default for the purpose of docker stats ls output. If the docker stats command is used and the "--format" flag is not provided with it, the docker client will automatically refer to the statsFormat property for this purpose. If the statsFormat property has not been set, then the docker client will then refer instead to the default table format for this purpose.

secretFormat: The "secretFormat" property will specify the format that is used by default for the purpose of docker secret ls output. If the docker secret ls command is used and the "--format" flag is not provided with it, the docker client will automatically refer to the secretFormat property for this purpose. If the secretFormat property has not been set, then the docker client will then refer instead to the default table format for this purpose.

nodesFormat: The "nodesFormat" property will specify the format that is used by default for the purpose of docker node ls output. If the docker node ls command is used and the "--format" flag is not provided with it, the docker client will automatically refer to the nodesFormat property and will use the value of the nodesFormat for this purpose. If the nodesFormat property has not been set with a value, then the docker client will then refer instead to the default table format for this purpose.

configFormat: The "configFormat" property will specify the format that is used by default for the purpose of docker config ls output. If the docker config ls command is used and the "--format" flag is not provided with it, the docker client will automatically refer to the configFormat property for this purpose. If the configFormat property has not been set, then the docker client will then refer instead to the default table format for this purpose.

credsStore: the "credsStore" property will specify an external binary that will be used as the credential store by default. When the credsStore property has been set, docker login will automatically try to use the external binary that has been specified by "docker-credential-<value>" for the purpose of storing credentials. This binary can be easily viewed within $PATH. If the credsStore property has not been set, then the docker client will then default to using the auths property of the config for the purpose of storing these credentials.

credHelpers: The "credHelpers" property will specify a group of credential helpers that will be used by default for the purposes of storing or retrieving credentials for specific registries. These credential helpers will automatically take priority over the credsStore property or auths for the purposes of the storage and retrieval of any relevant credentials. If the credHelpers property has not been set, then the docker client will then refer instead to the docker-credential-<value> binary by default for the purposes of the storage or retrieval of any relevant credentials for specific registries.

stackOrchestrator. The "stackOrhestrator" property will specify the orchestrator that is used by default for the purpose of running any docker stack management commands. Values that will be considered valid for this purpose include "all," "kubernetes," "swarm." It is also possible to override this property by using the "--orchestrator" flag, or by using the "DOCKER_STACK_ORCHESTRATOR" environment variable.

More information about all of these properties and various other useful features can be found within the relevant sections of the docker login documentation, as well.

Chapter 9: Docker Engine

The next topic that will be important to discuss when you are attempting to master docker is the Docker Engine. This was discussed briefly in an earlier chapter of this book but will be covered in more detail here, as well. The Docker engine can be described as a platform meant to help developers to create, run, and ship various applications. When people say "Docker," they are usually either referring to the company called Docker, or the product created by the Docker company, called the Docker Engine. The Docker engine allows its users to create and run applications, which are largely separate from their system's infrastructure by using containers. These containers can allow applications to run consistently, regardless of the system that they are being run on. By using the Docker Engine's unique methods of testing, shipping, and deploying your applications, you can significantly reduce the time that it takes to create container-based applications that run efficiently regardless of the system.

Docker can give its users the ability to pack up an application into a largely isolated (or contained) environment, which is referred to as a container, and then run that application from the container. This isolation can provide extra security as well as making it easier for you to run multiple different containers at the same time on a particular system. Containers can be very "lightweight" because of their ability to be run directly within the kernel of the machine that they are being hosted on, which eliminates the need for a hypervisor. This is a very helpful feature and is what allows for multiple different containers to be run on a single system much more efficiently than if the applications were being run from their own separate virtual machines. You can imagine how much more taxing this can be on a single machine as opposed to simply being able to run each application on its own. Docker containers are even able to be run inside virtual machines acting as their hosts if a user required this capability.

Docker can help to speed up the development lifecycle and make the development of these applications even more efficient by enabling developers to create applications within standardized environments by using local containers for various applications and services. This can make containers especially helpful to workflows that rely on continuous integration or continuous delivery, as well.

The Docker Engine can also allow for much more portable workloads than any other product or service on the market with its container-based platform. With these containers, Docker's users can run applications on a wide variety of different environments, such as a developer's personal computer, a virtual machine in a data center, or even on a cloud provider. Docker's unique container-based platform and its portable nature make it much easier to manage all of your applications effectively and efficiently.

The Docker Engine's architecture relies on a client-server relationship. The Docker client will communicate with the docker "daemon," which is what actually does most of the work involving your docker containers. The docker daemon does not have to run on the same system, although it can definitely do that as well. The docker client is capable of connecting to a remote docker daemon, meaning that they can also be run on different systems if you choose to run them this way. This is because the Docker daemon will communicate with your client by using a REST API over a network interface. The Docker darmon is able to "listen" for requests from the Docker API and manage various objects such as containers, images, networks, and volumes within Docker as well. The Docker Daemon can even communicate with other darmons just as it communicates with your client in order to more effectively manage various services provided by Docker. Of course, the primary way that the docker daemon will be useful to you is through the docker client. The client is the main way that you will be able to make use of the daemon. When you use a command within the docker client, it will then send that command to the daemon, which will then process and complete those commands. It can also be helpful to note that a single Docker client is able to communicate with multiple daemons, in the same way, that the daemon can communicate with other daemons as well.

Another very useful feature of the Docker Engine is the registry. Docker registries are spaces that are used to store various docker container images. The Docker Hub and Docker Cloud are good examples of public registries. These services can be used by anyone. Docker is even specifically programmed to default to the Docker Hub when it searches for specific container images. While there are public registries that you can gain access to and use if you wish, you can also choose to create and run your own private ones, as well. If you use the "docker pull" or the "docker run" command, the images that you need will then be retrieved from the registry that you have configured. The "docker push" command will, of course, push an image to the registry that you have configured.

Chapter 10: Docker Swarm

The next topic that will need to be understood in order to gain a complete mastery of Docker and its products is the swarm. Most of Docker's other features function with a single host, being your own local machine, but docker can also be switched into a "swarm mode." A "swarm" can be described as a collection of machines that are all running docker simultaneously. Once these machines have all been clustered together, you can continue to run docker commands as normal, but they will need to be executed within the cluster by the swarm manager. The swarm manager is the only machine within a specific cluster that is able to execute commands made within the cluster, and is also exclusively able to bring additional machines into the cluster as "workers." When you activate the swarm mode on a specific machine, that machine will automatically become the manager of its swarm, with a collection of additional worker machines. A worker machine, of course, can not execute any commands or tell other machines what they can and can not do. The worker machine exists inside the cluster exclusively to provide a little bit of extra capacity.

These "worker" machines are typically referred to as "nodes," or "Docker nodes." While it is possible to run a single node or even multiple nodes from a single physical machine or from a cloud server, most docker swarm deployments are typically made up of several docker nodes that have been divided across multiple machines of these kinds. If a worker node wants to deploy a specific application within a swarm that it is a part of, they will need to submit a service definition to the swarm's manager. The manager will then need to send small units of work to be done (these are referred to as "tasks") to the worker nodes within the swarm. Once these tasks have been distributed to the worker nodes, and they have been received, the worker nodes can begin to execute the tasks that they have been assigned. This will include the manager nodes as well, as they are also set by default to function as worker nodes as well as swarm managers. However, it is possible to configure their settings and have them function exclusively as manager nodes. The tasks assigned to each node are monitored by an assigned agent, and the current states of each of the swarm's worker nodes will be reported to the manager in order to help the swarm manager to maintain an ideal state within the swarm.

One of the most significant advantages of using the swarm mode with docker instead of a single machine is the ability to alter or change the configuration of a specific service without having to restart that service manually. Docker will simply update this configuration automatically. Once the configuration has been updated, all of the service's current tasks that use the original one will be stopped, and then recreated with the new and updated configuration. Additionally, the swarm manager can set an "optimal state" for their swarm at the time of the swarm's creation, and docker will then manage the swarm in order to maintain that state as consistently as possible within the swarm. If one of the swarm's worker nodes becomes unavailable for some reason, then Docker will automatically redistribute all of the tasks that were assigned to that worker node to other worker nodes within the swarm. You can also run additional standalone docker containers along with any swarm services that are being run while running in swarm mode. Any Docker daemon is capable of serving in a swarm as a manager or a worker, or both simultaneously, and while swarm services can only be managed by the swarm's manager, standalone docker containers are able to be run from any daemon.

The Docker Swarm is centered primarily around the tasks that are divided up amongst and carried out by the manager and worker nodes within the swarm. These tasks are most often referred to as "services," and they function as the main basis of any interaction that occurs between the user and the Docker swarm itself. When a service is created, it will ask for you to specify the container image that you would like to use, as well as the specific commands that will be executed within any containers that are being run by the service. There are different ays that tasks can be divided up among the nodes within a particular swarm, as well. For example, wif a "replicated services" model is used, then the swarm's manager will distribute a particular number of "replica tasks" to all of the worker nodes that exist within the swarm. This number is based on the scale that was set for the swarm's desired state. In the case of a global service model, the swarm will distribute tasks for the service that is being run evenly among each node within the cluster that is available at the time of distribution. Each available node will receive one task with this kind of service model. Each task that is assigned to a worker node will carry with it its own docker container, and all of the specific commands that it will need to run inside that container, as well. The manager node will assign these tasks to the worker nodes based on the number of replicas that have been set within the service scale. Additionally, a task can not be transferred to another node once it has been assigned. The task can only be run on the node that it was assigned to. Otherwise, it will fail.

Additionally, it can be important to note for these purposes that you do have the option to use the Docker Desktop application for Mac or for Windows in order to test the features of swarm mode that deal with single nodes. This includes the initialization of a single node swarm, as well as the creation and scaling of various services. Docker "Moby" and "Hyper-V" will function as the single node swarms for Mac and Windows operating systems, respectively. However, it is currently not possible for the Docker Desktop application to test a swarm with multiple nodes on its own. This applies to both the Mac and Windows versions of Docker Desktop, as well.

You are allowed to use the Docker Machine that has been included with these applications in order to create the swarm nodes that you will need. You can run your commands from the Docker Desktop application on a Mac or Windows host, but that host itself is not able to participate in the swarm that is created. Once the swarm's nodes have been created, you will be able to run all of the swarm commands as they are shown in the Mac Terminal or Windows PowerShell, as long as the Docker Desktop application stays running.

Conclusion

Congratulations! At this point, you should have a much better idea of Docker and all of its various products and services, as well as how to use those products and services to help you to maximize your efficiency in building and running container-based applications.

This step by step guide to learning and mastering Docker has been designed to help you do exactly what it says on the cover; learn and master Docker. This incredibly helpful book is meant to serve as your guide in understanding many of the various different products and services that Docker offers to its users, as well as a number of the different features that exist within those products and services and how to use them as effectively as possible in order to maximize the benefits of using this incredibly unique service. Additionally, this book has gone over all of the little ins and outs of the Docker platform and its various products and services, including some tips, tricks, and shortcuts to help you even further in this goal.

This book went over a number of different topics to give you all of the tools necessary to gain a complete understanding and mastery over Docker's various products and services. These topics included things like the various reasons why you would (and should) choose Docker over any other possibly similar service as well as some short introductions and guides to many of the various products and services that docker offers to its users such as Docker Enterprise and Docker Desktop for Mac or Windows, and the Docker Hub. This book also went over many of the different features of Docker's various products and services, as well as how to actually use them at a fundamental level in order to help you to master this incredibly innovative platform for building and running applications as smoothly and efficiently as possible.

With all of that said and out of the way, I would like to offer one last word of gratitude to you for taking the initiative and purchasing this book, and another short congratulation for taking the steps necessary to understand and master the Docker platform and its various services. At this point, you should have all of the tools necessary to help you to learn how to use Docker's products and services as effectively as possible and to get the most out of these very innovative tools.

www.ingramcontent.com/pod-product-compliance
Lightning Source LLC
Chambersburg PA
CBHW071138050326

40690CB00008B/1498